I0503338

Table of Contents

Legal Disclaimer

Forward

Thank you for purchasing MS Word Fillable Forms. There is a lot of great information within the pages of this book. We will make it a very easy process and will build on your knowledge chapter by chapter.

I have 20 plus years working in top-tier law firms in New York City. You also know I love helping people with start-ups and teaching them how to do many of the things that people traditionally run to others to do for them. In short, this line of books enables people to wear many hats by providing high level training that anyone can benefit from and then take advantage of.

We will thoroughly explore MS Word Fillable Forms in that we will go over the original package referred to as the **Legacy Package**, and we will also go over the **Content Control Package** that came into being from MS Word 2007 onward. In this book I am not programming nor am I doing Visual Basic.

Whether you are a business owner who needs to generate your own forms, a secretary or word processing operator working in a corporation that generates their own forms or an individual working on his/her own and who offers the service of creating Fillable Forms this book will be quite valuable to you.

When you are done with this book, you will be very comfortable with the subject of MS Word Fillable Forms. These are skills that professionals pay document production specialists top dollar to do both quickly and accurately.

With that being said, let us learn how to create Fillable Forms in MS Word so you can do it as well!

Louis.

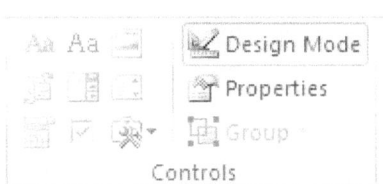

The focus of this book is going to be going over the use of the **Legacy** package (the original fillable forms package) and the newer **Content Control** package. I want to keep this book at a level where one can make use of the information right away without getting too deep in terms of programming etc. This book is going to help you whether you are **in business** or whether you are working in a **law firm or word processing center**. This is a great skill to have because even as a independent worker, you can solicit business for those companies that wish to automate their forms. Any way you look at it, this is a great skill to have.

You would be very surprised that many people still are using the typewriter in order to do their forms. I have nothing against the typewriter for I am from that era, but when you have to have other people outside of your company fill out a form and get it back to you quickly, fillable forms in MS Word, Adobe or Nuance makes the most sense since immediately upon finishing the form, they have the ability to either print it out and fax it or save it as a PDF and email to you. Point being that an intricate form can be filled out very quickly so this is obviously the way to go.

As to the "**Active X Controls**" which sits on the bottom row of the **Legacy Tools**, I am not going to deal with them in this book but here is what they refer to. The Active X is not a programming language, but instead, a set of rules for how an application should share information. Programmers develop Active X Controls using programming languages such as C, C+ Visual Basic and Java. The Active X Controls are similar to a Java Applet but they unlike the Java Applet, they have full access to the Windows Operating System. Active X Controls are written to work on Windows environments and Microsoft has developed a registration system so that Windows can identify and authenticate an Active X Control before it allows it to be downloaded. That is Active X in a nutshell, but for the purposes of this book, we do not have to get involved with it in order to set up the forms we will be dealing with. So, let me give you an additional skill you can now offer to others and for the business people you can create your own forms as needed.

I. TURNING ON YOUR DEVELOPER TAB

First we will discuss turning on the Developer Tab in MS Word 2007. If you look below, you click on the Microsoft Button and go to "Word Options". Under Word Options, you then go to "Popular" and you place a check next to "Show Developer Tab in the Ribbon". When you go back to the normal screen you will now see your Developer Tab now available for use.

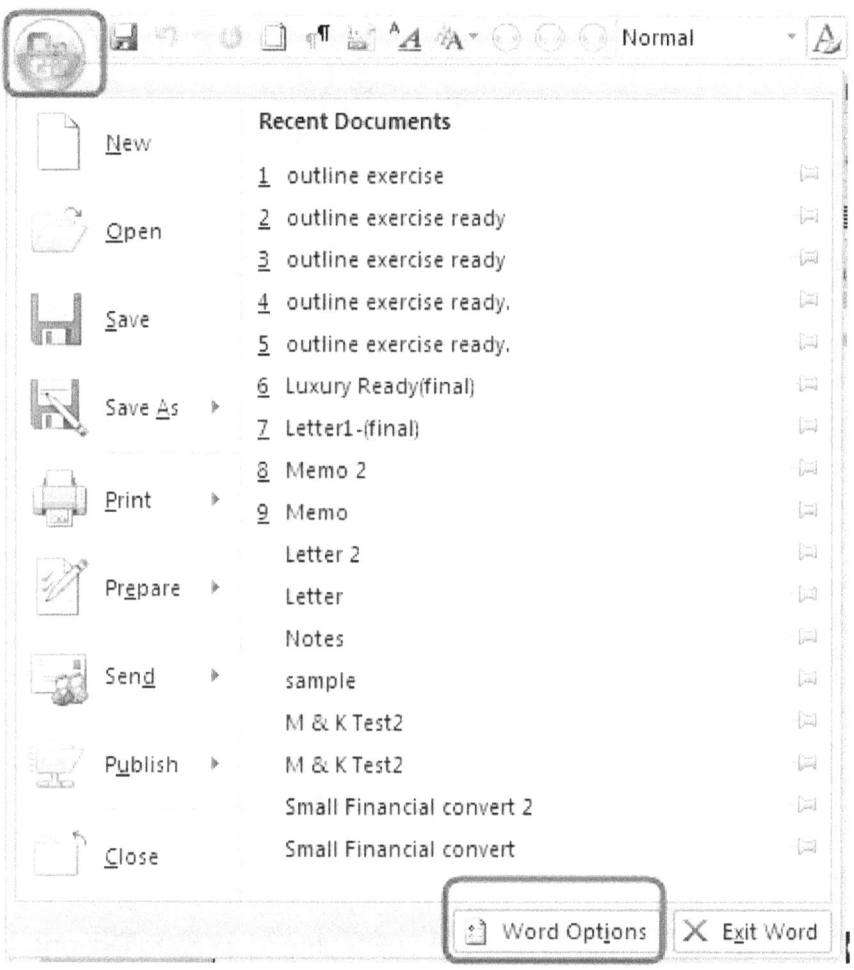

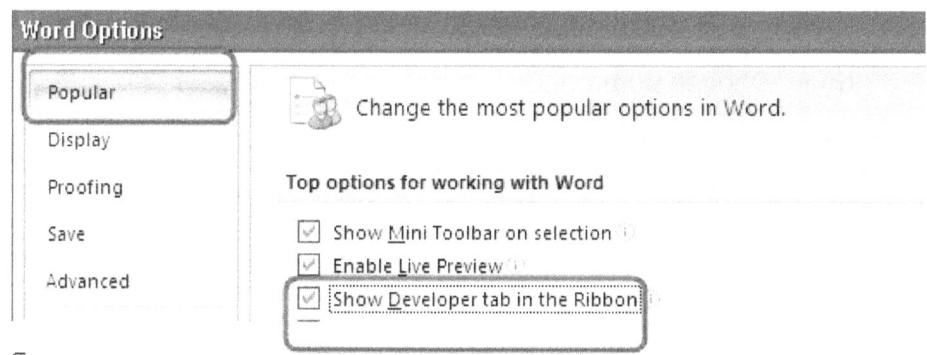

Second, we will now discuss how to **activate** the **Developer Tab in MS Word 2010-13**. In **MS Word 2010-13** go to **File, Options** and choose **Customize Ribbon**. Under **Customize the Ribbon**, you will see a choice of **Main Tabs**. Click the **Developer Tab** for sure toward the bottom and, if you wish to customize the Developer Tab, you can click on the "Developer (Custom) if you wish. *There are many YouTube videos that will take you through customizing a particular tab in MS Word 2007-13*. For our purposes, we want the Basics being **Legacy and Content Control** so just turning on the Developer Tab is fine for us. Make sure to click on **Okay** at the bottom of the screen for your selections to take effect.

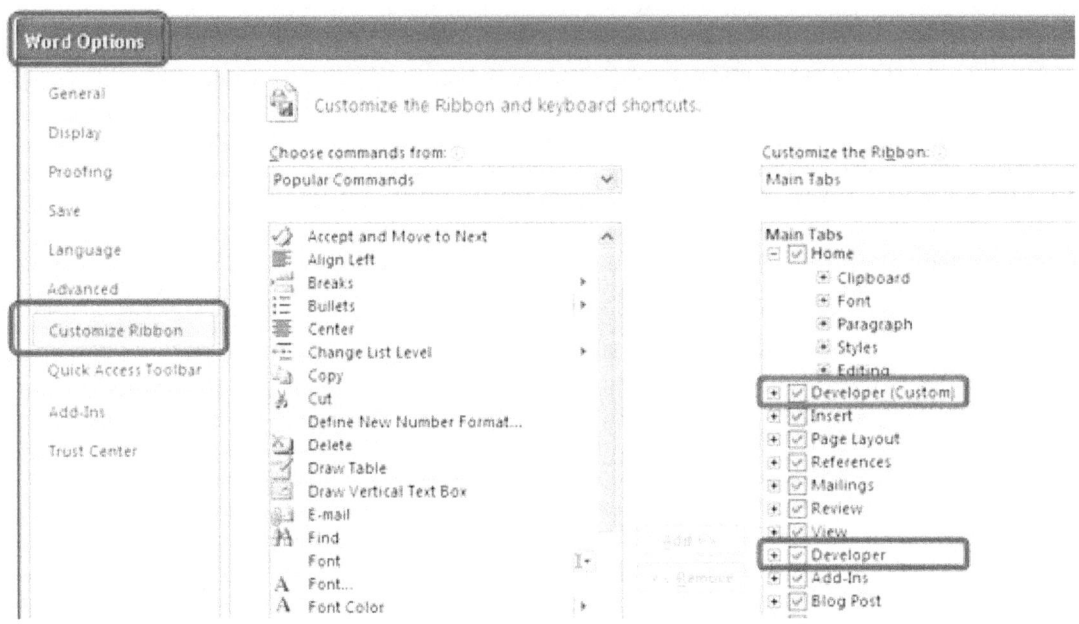

II.   ADDING THE LEGACY TOOLS FOLDER TO YOUR QUICK ACCESS TOOLBAR

If you wish to add the Legacy Forms folder to your quick access tool bar then do the following:

1.   Go to Microsoft Button (**2007**) or **File** and then go to **Options**.

2.   Under Options, choose **Quick Access Toolbar.**

3.   Under **Choose Commands From** choose "**Developer Tab**".

4.   When you get the list of the items under the Developer Tab, look for the yellow **Legacy Tool Folder** and add it to the **right side** which represents what is **currently** sitting in your **Quick Access Toolbar**. When you are done, and you look up at your quick access toolbar, you will now see your Legacy Tools waiting for you. If you do a lot of Forms creation, then you might wish to do this. It will save you a step.

III. GOING OVER THE LEGACY FORMS

In terms of using the Legacy tools, we can work in a **Word 97–2003** document with no problem. If we choose to also make use of the newer fillable forms that came about from 2007-13, then in order to activiate the newer tools so we can make use of them, we then need to save our file as a 2007, 2010 or 2013. **Macro Enabled Word Document** or a **Macro Enabled Template is also used for this newer package.** Right now, we are **strickly going to deal with the Legacy** (the older method), so we **do not** need to save the file as anything more than MS Word 97-2003. Let us now start the process of identifying the different pieces of the **Legacy Tool Box** so to speak. Legacy Forms are easy to use so we will go through the pieces then we will apply the pieces to the forms. It is an easy process so let us have some fun and proceed.

IV. THE TEXT FORM FIELD.

The **Text Form Field** will allow the user of the form to **hop from one area that needs us to type text into it to another.** It lets you hop from one field to another by use of the **tab button.** When you set up a fillable form and we make use of the **Text Form Field** whether it be the **Legacy** or the **newer version**, we **lock** the document down so the textual portion that is **"not" part of the fillable portion of the form** is **not accessible** to the user of the form. Therefore, the form cannot be altered but rather, the areas that need to be filled in can be and **that is all that can be affected.** So, let us place our first text field in. Below we have the initial piece of a loan agreement and we can go over placing the Text Fields in their proper locations.

This MULTIFAMILY MORTGAGE, ASSIGNMENT OF LEASES AND RENTS, SECURITY AGREEMENT AND FIXTURE FILING (as amended, restated, replaced, supplemented, or otherwise modified from time to time, the "Security Instrument") dated as of _____, is executed by [IF BORROWER IS AN ENTITY: _____, a _____ organized and existing under the laws of _____] OR [IF BORROWER IS AN INDIVIDUAL: _____, a [married][single] individual], as mortgagor ("Borrower"), to and for the benefit of _____, a _____ organized and existing under the laws of _____, as mortgagee ("Lender").

We will insert in the form field at the various locations and we will also set it up to underscore as we place in the needed text.

1.	The first area we see is "dated as of _____" as shown in the highlighted area above. So highlight the underscore after the words "dated as of" and go to your **Developer Tab**.

2.	You **don't need** to turn on **Design Mode** if working in the Legacy package.

3.	Go to your Legacy tools. (Yellow Folder)

4.	In the Legacy Tools folder choose the Text Form Field Icon (**ab**).

5.	In comes your Text Form Field (looks like this) where you can click on it and select underscore as shown in the picture below (the field is underscored). If you **do not** want the area that the recipient needs to fill in to be **underscored**, then simply bring in the Field as is.

This MULTIFAMILY MORTGAGE, ASSIGNMENT OF LEASES AND RENTS, SECURITY AGREEMENT AND FIXTURE FILING (as amended, restated, replaced, supplemented, or otherwise modified from time to time, the "Security Instrument") dated as of , is executed by.....

6.	Again, I reiterate that some people **want** the areas that the client fills out to be **underscored** while others are happy to get the needed information keyed in and **do not** want it underscored. Now, let us insert the field codes to the rest of the paragraph. Remember, as you insert your field codes, remember to remove bracketed information (provided you know the exact situation of the recipient) since they were only placed in the document as guides to those variable items that needed text to be inserted such as Individual or Corporation, Single or Married etc.

This MULTIFAMILY MORTGAGE, ASSIGNMENT OF LEASES AND RENTS, SECURITY AGREEMENT AND FIXTURE FILING (as amended, restated, replaced, supplemented, or otherwise modified from time to time, the "Security Instrument") dated as of , is executed by [IF BORROWER IS AN ENTITY: , a , organized and existing under the laws of . OR [IF BORROWER IS AN INDIVIDUAL: , a [married][single] individual], as mortgagor ("Borrower"), to and for the benefit of , a organized and existing under the laws of , as mortgagee ("Lender").¶

7.	Okay, so let's keep moving. Let us say that the paragraph above represents what we **needed** to prepare in terms of the Text Form Fields for the fillable section of the document. So after putting in the Text Form Fields, what do we do next to actually make this an active fillable form?

8.	In your Developer Tab, turn **off** your "**Design Mode" button if on**. You don't need the Design Mode button to be on to use the Legacy system.

9.	Click on **Restrict Editing**.

10.   After you click on "**Restrict Editing**", up comes the "**Restrict Formatting and Editing Panel** on the right side of your screen as shown on the form below.

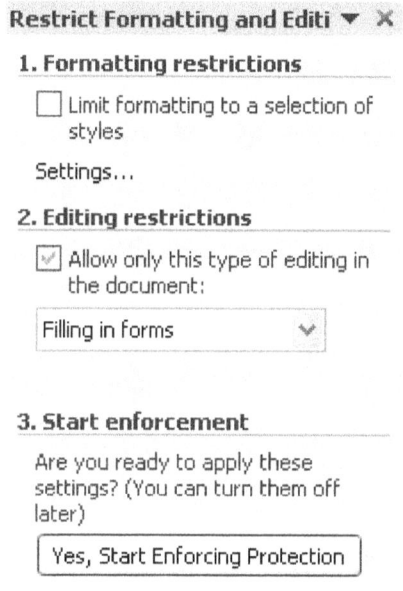

11.   Choose **No. 2** and choose "**Filling In Forms**"

12.   Now choose **Yes, Start Enforcing Protection**

13.   Upon clicking Yes, Start Enforcing Protection, You will get a prompt to put in a Password.

14.   If you are in the **development mode** and are still tinkering with the form and you simply wish to test the form **use a one digit (letter or number) for the password**. In this way, you will have much less of a liklihood that you will **accidentally forget** the password. Believe me, it happens a lot. When you are ready to lock it down for good and send the form to the intended recipient, you then place a traditional password but make sure you write down what you used, otherwise, you will never be able to unlock the form for editing again. The Password dialog box looks like the one below: **Very important: Carefully read** NO. 20 **of this section for some great relief info regarding the password aspect.**

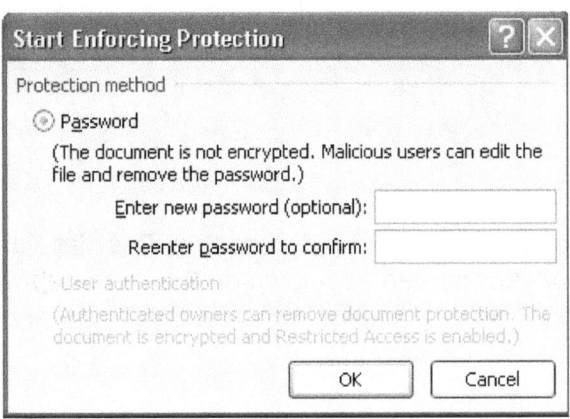

15.   After you put in your one digit password, proceed to hop through all of the text form fields to see 1) whether you can fill text as intended and 2) make sure that there is sufficient space between the form field and the words that proceed and the words that follow. If not, when you unlock the form, you can then put in **proper space if need be** after or before a particular field.

16.   To **unlock the form** so that you may **go back to editing the form**, you will do the following: Click on your **Developer Tab**. Do not click on "**Design Mode**".

17.   Click on "**Restrict Editing**" (if the panel if **not** already visible on the right side).

18.   On the right side panel a message will come up that says:

19.   Click on **Stop Protection** and put in your password to open up the form for editing.

Note: After you unlock the form, before you continue working on the form, click on the "**Reset Form Fields Button** ✎ within the Legacy Tools folder to clear out any text you may have placed in the Form Fields so that your fields are back to their original pristine condition.

20.   VERY IMPORTANT!: While some people will want to place that one digit password while in development so that someone else (who you may send it to for testing) does not have access to the text of the form without your permission, you should know the following: When the system asks you to put in a password YOU DO NOT HAVE TO PUT ONE IN. YOU CAN JUST SAY "OKAY" AND THAT WILL PLACE THE DOCUMENT IN LOCK MODE SO YOU CAN QUICKLY TEST YOUR FORM. WHEN YOU WANT TO UNDO THE LOCK MODE, JUST CLICK ON RESTRICT EDITING (IF YOUR RIGHT SIDE PANEL IS NOT ALREADY UP) AND JUST CLICK ON STOP PROTECTION TO UNLOCK. THIS PERTAINS TO ANY TIME YOU NEED TO LOCK THE FORM QUICKLY AND TEST IT. WHEN YOU ARE READY TO ACTUALLY DISTRIBUTE THE FORM, YOU CAN THEN MAKE SURE YOU DO A FULL PASSWORD AND MAKE SURE TO RECORD IT IN A SAFE PLACE.

V.   TEXT FORM FIELD OPTIONS

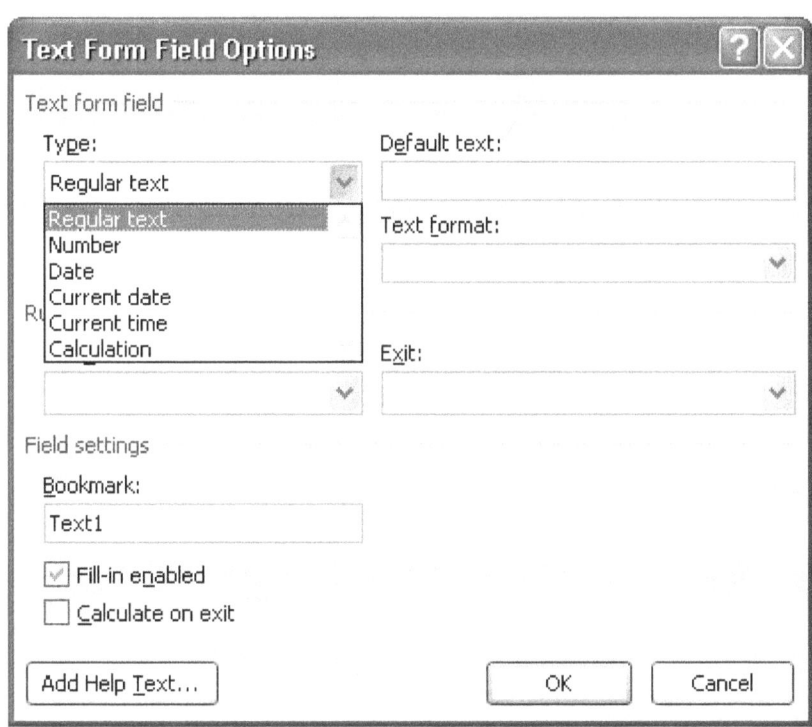

Before we move on I wish to go through some of the controls that are available concerning the **Legacy Text Field Code**. If you click on a particular Text Field Code, it will turn Blue. [image]. You can either right click on the field code and go to **Properties** or you can, in your Developer Tab, go to **Properties** under your "Design Mode" button. In the Legacy package, just so you know, **you don't have to** have your **Design Mode button** on in order to enter the Properties for a particular Text Form field.

1.   Under the Text Form Field Properties section we will look at the "**Text Form Field Options Dialog Box**" first. As you can see above, under "**Type**", we can determine what type of text we wish to **allow to be inserted** on **any particular Text Form Field**. Obviously. the choice of **Regular Text** will be the majority of uses but, we

can see that we can have the user only be able to insert numbers, the date, the time etc.

       2.   Under "**Default Text**" we can type in text that we want the user to see before they type in their text so it would look like this: INSERT·YOUR·COMPANY·NAME. It should be noted that after they are finished, typing in the text on the form field that had the "**Default Text**" waiting for them, they will have to back out (delete) any excess Default text after they **type in the intended text** or they can first highlight the Default Text and then type in what they need to type to replace the Default text. Either way will work.

       3.   For "**Text Format**", you have a number of options of how you can control the look of the text as you see below.

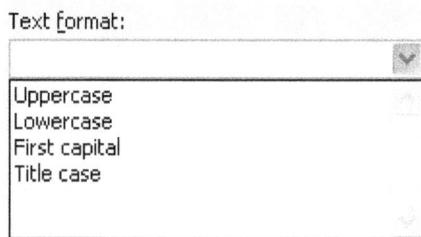

       4.   For **Calculate On Exit** here is the scoop.

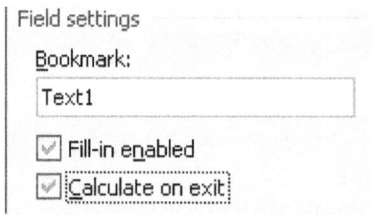

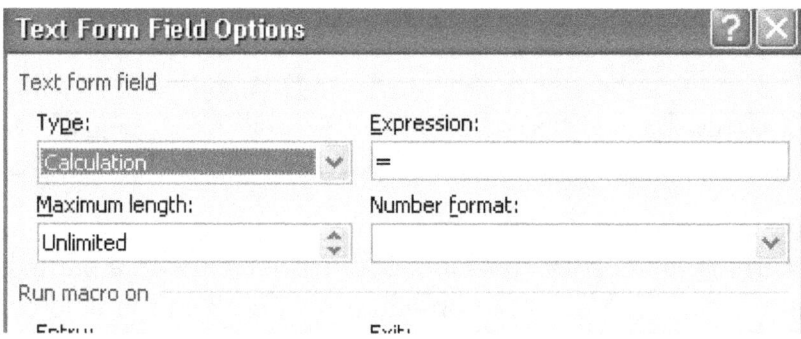

a) On the Legacy Tools click the **Text Form Field Button** ![abl] to insert a Text Form Field and then press **ENTER**.

b) Insert **two additional Text Form Fields** and follow with **ENTER** after each one as well.

c) Right click on the first Form Field and go to **Properties**. For that field under "**Type**" select "**Number**", under Field Settings, make sure "Calculate on exit" is checked. Repeat the same for the second form field.

d) For the **third** Form Field go to options and under "Type" select "Calculation". Up comes a different set of choices for the Text Form Field Options. For "Expression" type **=SUM(Text1,Text2)** and click **OK**. As you can see, the **first two** Text Form Fields have bookmark names of Text1 and Text2. Capitalization counts here. In this example, the **Expression** results in the **sum** of the first two form fields.

5.　　Let us wrap up this particular area of the Text Form Field Options Dialog Box by discussing "**Add Help Text**". Similar in nature to "**Default Text**", this feature lets you guide the user through the form by placing helpful **instructional text** for the user. This text will show up in the **Status Bar** at the bottom of your screen.

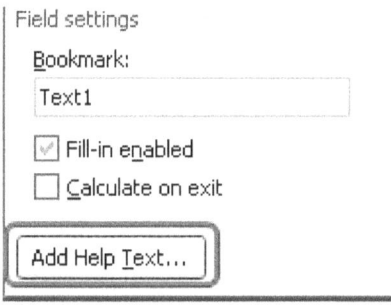

6.　　So, click on "**Add Help Text**" and type in the help text that you want the user to see for **that particular** Text Field.

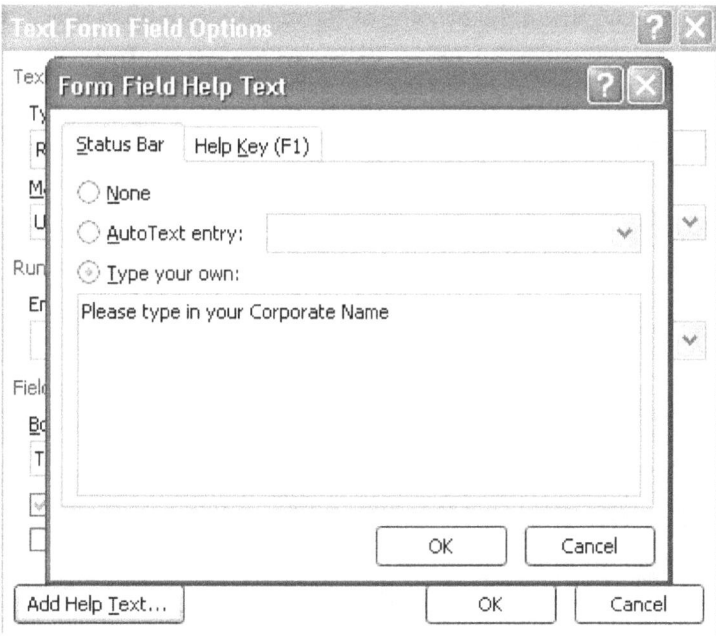

7.	Now you would go through the process of password protecting the form and when you come across the area of your form that has Instructional Help Text you will see the following in the Status Bar.

Please type in your Corporate Name

For the **Legacy** routine, this is basically it so what we will do is to now add to the routine by introducing more Field Types from the Legacy Tools Folder. Don't worry about the routine, I will keep going over it for each Field Type we explore.

## VI.	THE CHECKBOX

Now that we have the basic routine concerning the use of the Legacy Forms Tools, let us now look at the check box. It is simple enough. Let's look at the example below:

Red¤	☐¤	¤
Blue¤	☒¤	¤
Yellow¤	☐¤	¤

So above, we have a situation whereby the recipient is asked to make a choice of three colors. The choice of Blue has been made. They could have made the choice of all 3 since each of the independent check boxes (**which result in an X**) do not depend on each other. So, again, to insert the check boxes and then test your form you would:

1.	Go to your Developer Tab

2.	Click on the Legacy Tools Folder.

3.	Click on the Check Box Form Field to produce the check box where needed.

4.	After you have inserted your check boxes click on Restrict Editing

5.	Under Editing restrictions, (No. 2) choose Filling in Forms.

6.	Click the "**Yes, Start Enforcing Protection button**" and put in your **password or just say OKAY.**

7. Test your form and to get back to edit the form, click on **Restrict Editing** again (if the right panel is not already on) and click the Stop Protection Button

8. Put in your **Password** (if you used one) or if not, just click "**Stop Protection**" and **continue to edit your form**.

9. The controls for the check box work very similar to that of the Text Form Field. ☐. **Double Click** or **right click and choose** Properties in order to get into the **Check Box Properties**.

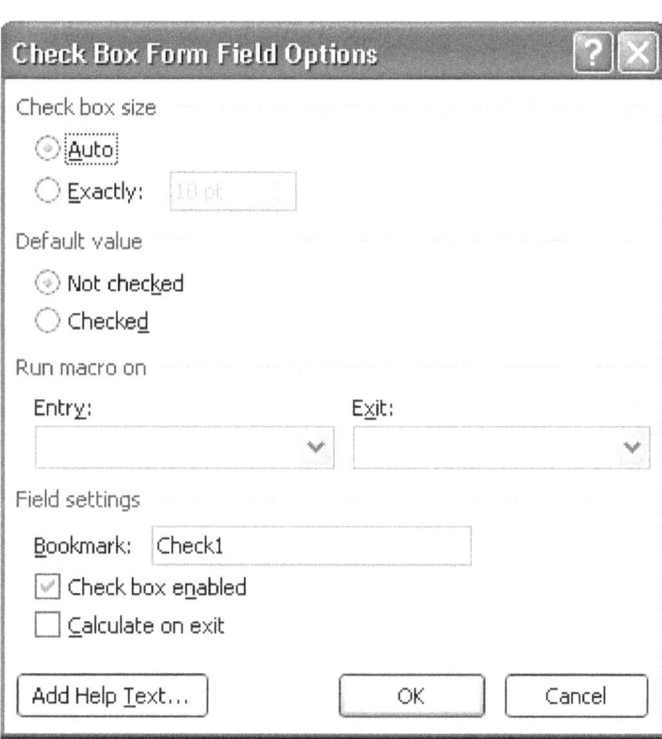

10. As you can see above, the Check Box Form Field Options. Take note, that I usually choose "**Auto**" so that the size of my check box **will match** the current font size of the document. Also, remember to make sure that "**Check box enabled**" is selected otherwise, it will **not** work.

VII.   THE DROP DOWN FORM FIELD

Moving right along, we now come across the **Drop Down Menu**. Easy to use, Easy to Implement.

1.   Go to your Developer Tab

2.   Click on the Legacy Tools Folder.

3.   Click on the Drop Down Form Field to produce the Drop Down Menu Field Code.

It looks like this:

When you first bring in the Drop Down Form Field **double click** on it to bring up the Dialog Box to **add** all of your items that will be listed in the **Drop Down Menu**.

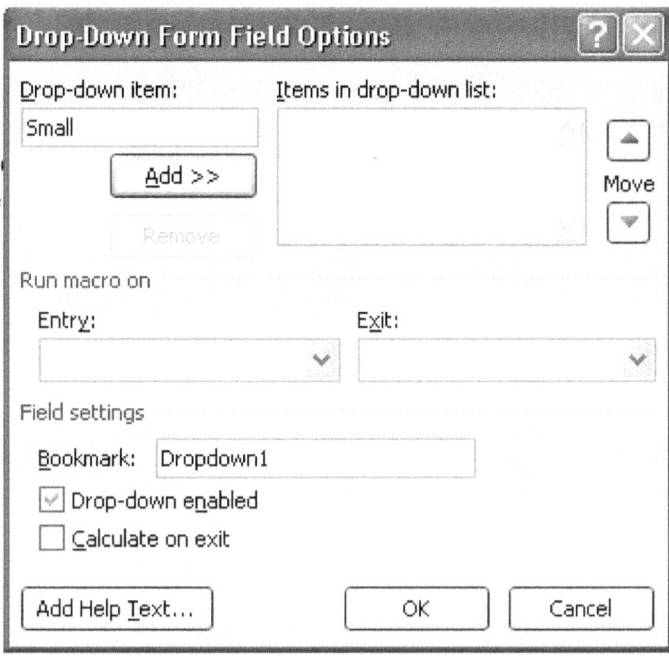

4.   Proceed to type in the items that will make up your Drop Down Menu. Type each item in the "Drop-down item:" selection and press Add.

5.   Make sure **Drop-down enabled** box is checked.

6.   Add Help Text if you wish such as *"**Make Your Choice**"*

7.   Once all of the items have been input it will look like the picture below:

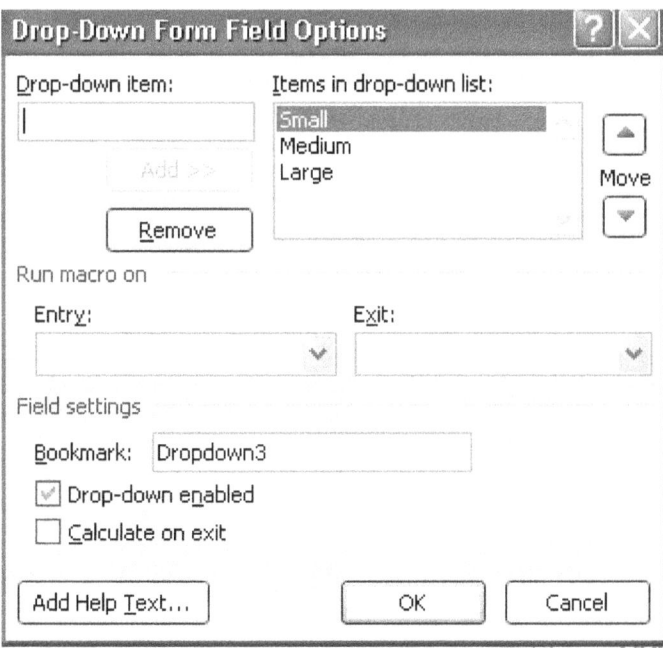

8.   Check to see that it is working. First click on Restrict Editing

9. Under Editing restrictions, (No. 2) choose Filling in Forms.

10. Click the **Ýes, Start Enforcing Protection button** and put in your **password if you need to use one or just click OKAY**.

11. Test your form and to get back to edit the form, click on **Restrict Editing** again (if the panel is not active) and click the Stop Protection Button

12. Put in your **Password** if you used one, if not, *as soon as you click Stop Protection, the document will again be available* and **continue to edit your form**.

13. The Drop Down Menu piece of the form when ready to go should look like this within the document once it is protected. When the user of the form clicks on the form which will look something like the this "Small" they will then see the drop down portion as shown below once they click on it.

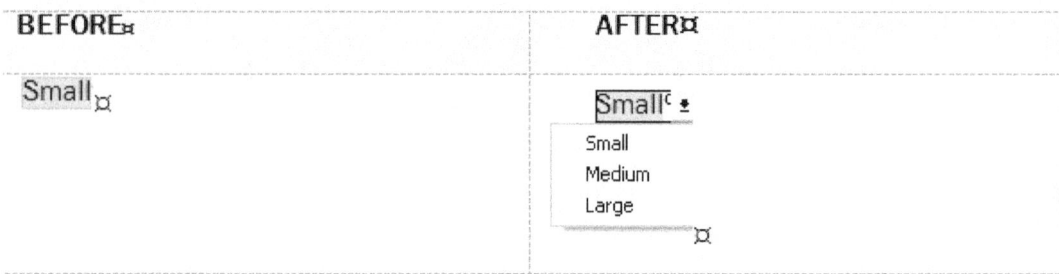

IX.   INSERT FRAME

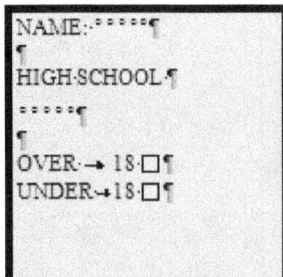

THE·ABC·COLLEGE·THE·ABC·COLLEGE·THE·ABC·
COLLEGE·THE·ABC·COLLEGE·THE·ABC·COLLEGE·
THE·ABC·COLLEGE·THE·ABC·COLLEGE·THE·ABC·
COLLEGE·THE·ABC·COLLEGE·THE·ABC·COLLEGE·
THE·ABC·COLLEGE·THE·ABC·COLLEGE·THE·ABC·
COLLEGE·THE·ABC·COLLEGE·THE·ABC·COLLEGE·
THE·ABC·COLLEGE·THE·ABC·COLLEGE·THE·ABC·
COLLEGE·THE·ABC·COLLEGE·THE·ABC·COLLEGE·
THE·ABC·COLLEGE·THE·ABC·COLLEGE·THE·ABC·COLLEGE·THE·ABC·
COLLEGE·THE·ABC·COLLEGE·THE·ABC·COLLEGE·THE·ABC·COLLEGE·

Here is the situation as to **Insert Frame**. For the most part. it can be used in order to create a look of how the text flows but besides controlling how text flows "**No Text Wrapping** or **Text Wrapping Around the Entire Box or** as we see above, we can use the Frame to Insert Other Legacy Forms which need to be filled in by the recipient.

1.   You can, within the Frame, insert the Text Form Field, the Check Box Form Field and the Drop Down Form Field. In my sample above, I inserted a Frame and, within the Frame, I put in Text Form Fields for the students to fill in as well as check boxes for them to check off as needed. Take note that I was also able to go to **Borders and Shading** and insert a background color to make the Frame a bit more interesting to look at.

2.   Once the students in my **mock example** get past the initial requests of the **test cover page**, they will read the questions within the test booklet and will select their answer A,B,C or D by using check boxes but the Frame that you see above, enabled me to get the look that you see. Some of you will say, **why did you not just use a text box since a text box can have the text surround it on both sides or one side under the layout options**? Yes, under ordinary circumstances, but text boxes **will not accept Legacy Form Fields** so that is why the **Frame** is used. Frames are used as the substitute for Text Boxes since they have the **capacity to hold Form Fields**.

3.   When you first insert your Frame, you can either double click on the lines of the Frame to open up the **Frames Dialog Box** or you can right click on the Frame and choose "**Format Frame**". You then see the following:

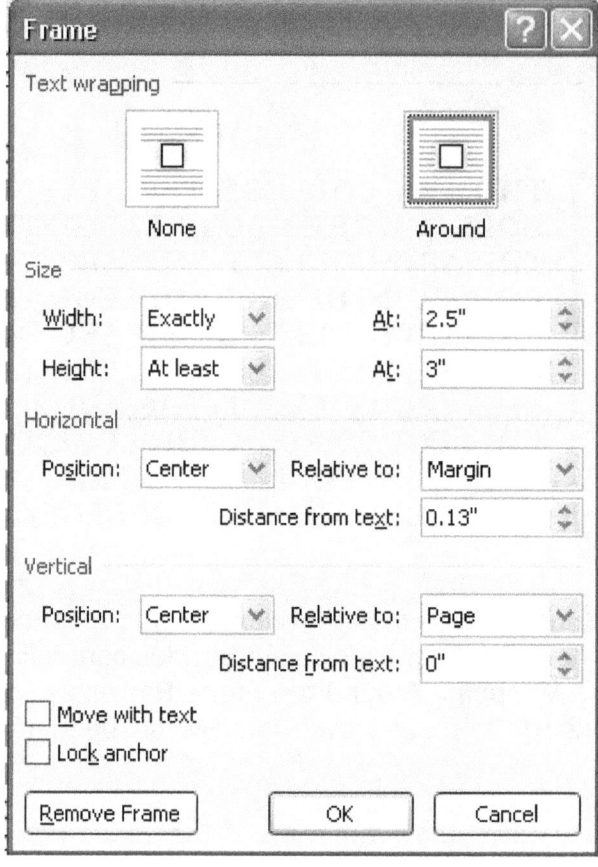

4.   Here you can control your Frames **Height** and **Width**, **Horizontal** vs **Vertical** position on the page. If the text is going to surround the box how close do you wish for the other text to come to the Frame and on and on. It is a nice tool that will allow you to take advantage of the Legacy Form Tools in a way that the regular Text Box can not.

5.   Okay, so let's say that you put in your frame, set your text, dropdowns and check boxes within the remainder of your document and are now ready to lock it down so it can now be used by the recipient or tested by you. Let us once again go through the routine.

A.   Click on your **Developer Tab**.

B.   Insert your frame and any other Legacy tools you need within your document.

C.   Within the Developer Tab click on "**Restrict Editing**"

D.   Under Editing Restrictions choose **No. 2** and choose **Filling in forms**

E.   Click **Yes, Start Enforcing Protection**

F.   Put in your **password or just say OKAY**. If this is a final, use a **real password and make note of it in a safe place.**

G.   If you want to go back to edit the form, under the Developer tab click **Restrict Editing** (if the right side panel is not already up) and click on "**Stop Protection**".

H.   If you used a password put in your password or if not just click "Stop Protection" and you are **back in business**. Go back to editing your forms document.

X.   FORM FIELD SHADING

We are coming towards the end of the Legacy forms and then we will head into the new set of forms that came in from MS Word 2007 on. Now, I recently did a job at a bank where my job was to totally reformat their loan documents using styles and multilevel outlining. Once I finished formatting all of the documents, they wanted me to then prepare all of their loan documents for fillable forms. One day, we were testing a particular form and although I was able to insert the Text Form Field, it would come in without the telltale shading and looks like this ° ° ° ° °. When we locked down the file, the cursor would hop from text form field to text form field but without the telltale shading it was not a comfortable experience to use in not seeing any of the form field areas.

In a work situation, where we were under some pressure, we, at the time, could not figure out why all of a sudden we were getting this ° ° ° ° ° instead of this ° ° ° ° °. So, I just wanted you to appreciate how a little thing like knowing how to put on the shading that envelopes the Text Form Field is accomplished. Now that you know what makes the form shaded, you will probably say wow, that is it? Keep in mind that I have seen many people think it was connected to regular Field Shading that is under **Format, Options, Advanced**. That field shading has to do with page numbering, list numbering, the completed Table of Contents, Table of Authorities, Index of Terms, Cross References, anything that has to do with automating the document. And that Field Shading should be set for **Always**. But, it will **not** control the Legacy Text Form Field. Knowing this tidbit will save you or some other individulal angst because you will know how to remedy it!

XII.   RESET FORM FIELDS

Legacy Forms

This has to do with clearing out the forms after you have tested them all the way through or partially through the document and they are in working order. You then want to clear out anything that you may have placed within the form so you are back to having all of your forms clear meaning a clean slate so to speak before you go back to editing or to lock it down for good to send to a target organization or individual.

1.   You Protect your form.

2.   Test your form. Louis|

3.   Stop the protection

4.   Reset your forms. °°°°° Go back to editing the form.

In Sum: When you are done with your form, you can do the following:

A.   You can save the finished fillable form as a template for people to use internally. In this way, they have to save to a new document and they can feed off of the template in perpetuity.

B.   When you send the locked form to someone, they can fill it out and save it. They can save it and/or print it as well. They can then take the print out and fax it if needed or can send the saved MS Word fillable form document back to you for you to print.

C.   The recipient can fill it out and save it and then email it to you or save it as a PDF and email it to you.

D.   If the recipient is a client who has to fill out that form on a regular basis, you may consider sending them the template version for them to use as well. They will welcome the chance to do everything on their computer and not have to look for a typewriter.

Before we move onto the new package, I just want to show you some small pieces of using forms.

Example 1: Taken from a Mortgage Agreement. Using the check box.

> **ATTACHED EXHIBITS.** The following Exhibits are attached to this Security Instrument and incorporated fully herein by reference:
>
> ☐   Exhibit A   Description of the Land (required)
>
> ☐   Exhibit B   Modifications to Security Instrument
>
> **[Remainder of Page Intentionally Blank]**

Example 2: Taken from the same Mortgage Agreement

Before the Forms Fields Were Inserted	After the Text Form Fields Were Inserted
BORROWER : By → _____ → _____(SEAL)¶ Name _____ → Title ◄_____ → ¶ The name, chief executive office and organizational identification number of Borrower (as Debtor under any applicable Uniform Commercial Code) are ¶ Debtor Name Record Owner _____ → Debtor Chief Executive Office Address ¶ _____ → ¶ _____ → ¶ _____ → ¶ Debtor Organizational ID Number _____ → ¶ [INSERT·BORROWER·NOTICE·ADDRESS·IF· DIFFERENT]o The name and chief executive office of Lender (as Secured Party) are ¶ Secured Party Name _____ → ¶ Secured Party Chief Executive Office Address ¶ _____ → ¶ _____ → ¶ _____ → ¶ [INSERT·LENDER·NOTICE·ADDRESS·IF· DIFFERENT]: ¶	BORROWER : By → °°°°°(SEAL)¶ Name °°°°°¶ Title →°°°°°¶ The name, chief executive office and organizational identification number of Borrower (as Debtor under any applicable Uniform Commercial Code) are ¶ Debtor Name RecordOwner °°°°°¶ Debtor Chief Executive Office Address ¶ °°°°°¶ °°°°°¶ °°°°°¶ Debtor Organizational ID Number °°°°°¶ [INSERT·BORROWER·NOTICE·ADDRESS·IF· DIFFERENT]o The name and chief executive office of Lender (as Secured Party) are ¶ Secured Party Name °°°°°¶ Secured Party Chief Executive Office Address ¶ °°°°°¶ °°°°°¶ °°°°°¶ ¶ [INSERT·LENDER·NOTICE·ADDRESS·IF· DIFFERENT]: °°°°°¶ °°°°°¶ °°°°°¶ ¶

Example 3: Signature Blocks

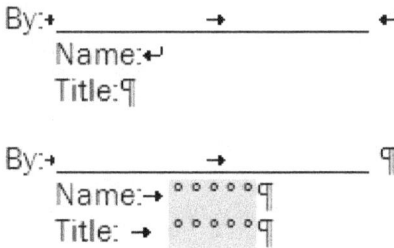

Finally, there is **Example 3 -** the signature block. The top block includes the graphic symbols so you can see how they are **normally handled in law firms. Note:** The use of soft returns and the fact that the first signature block is not set up for Text Fields. **Note:** The second signature block is slightly different in that I have placed **a hard return** after the signature line that was done using a **right tab in the ruler** with a **solid line leader** assigned to it. (*View Tab Dialog Box To See Solid Line Leader Selection*) and a hard return after both **Name:** and **Title:** with the Form Field following so that the recipient can type in the Name and Title and print it out and then sign with his/her signature after the word **By:**

The hard returns will lead to more stability of the signature blocks since the blocks would now be used in a fillable forms setting and not just dealt with by legal secretaries.

Yeah! You are done with Legacy. Let us now move on to the newer version.

XIII.   CONTENT CONTROLS

For this section you will have to make sure that you save your MS Word File as a **2007-13** so that you can activate the **newer controls** having to do with fillable forms.

Note that in the picture above, I clicked on the "Design Mode" button. This will give me access to the "**Properties**" section when I select a **particular** Field and wish to deal with the Dialog Box of a **particular** field.

The Design mode button, when on, will light up the properties selection underneath it.

Having it on, will also enable you to get to the properties dialog box of a particular form field of this newer set of form fields and if you **right click** on any of the new form fields, you can also go to properties.

Rich Text Content Control vs. Plain Text Content Control:

Rich Text Content Control contains text or other items such as tables, pictures or other content. It also holds text that the user can **optionally** format such as bold and italic. I will come back to this.

A **Plain Text Content Control** is one that we will deal with more fully for the purposes of this book. A Plain Text Content Control contains text alone. It cannot contain other items such as tables or pictures. It holds text that the user cannot format and is therefore guided by you by use of being able to use a style embedded into the form to control the Font, the Font size and any attributes we want to attach to the font such as bold or underscore or italic but are locked into what you provide for them.

Let us start out talking about the **Plain Text Content Control** that looks like the double A you see on this line. Aa.

Below is our sample of what we used in the first part of the book.

This MULTIFAMILY MORTGAGE, ASSIGNMENT OF LEASES AND RENTS, SECURITY AGREEMENT AND FIXTURE FILING (as amended, restated, replaced, supplemented, or otherwise modified from time to time, the "Security Instrument") dated as of ███████████, is executed by [IF BORROWER IS AN ENTITY: _____, a

1.   Take a look at the blue area above. (a) We will bring in a **Text Content Control Form Field**. Next, (b) we will make use of a **character style** that in this case, does nothing more than underscore text since in this situation, we have made the mock descision that those areas that the recipient fills in should be **underscored**, (c) we will also make sure that there is text **on the surface** of the Text Content Control form field that will alert (instruct) the recipient as to what we would like them to do for that particular area they are about to fill in. So, let us now go through the process. It is not hard at all. Besides having surface instructional text as an option, I will go over with you how to include instructional text in your dialog box as well if you want to instruct that way.

2.   Go to your **Developer Tab**. Make sure your **Design mode** button is on. Choose your **Plain Text Content Control Icon** for your Form Field Aa

3.   In   comes   your   **Plain   Text   Content   Control   Form**. Click here to enter text. :. If I did not have the "**Design Mode**" button pressed, then that same content control form field would look like this Click here to enter text . You should know right off the bat that **by Default**, a Text Form Field (Content Control Type) **takes on the paragraph formatting of whatever paragraph you should place it in**. I will **also be showing you how to embed a style in the form field** for **additional control of the look** beyond that of the **Default Text**.

4.   So, with your **Design Mode** button pressed, and your cursor within the new Text Field, let us take a look at the **properties** end of this button.

5.   Either go to "**Properties**" that sits under the words **Design Mode** in the **Developer Tab**

or right click on the Plain Text Content Control Form Field and choose **Properties**.

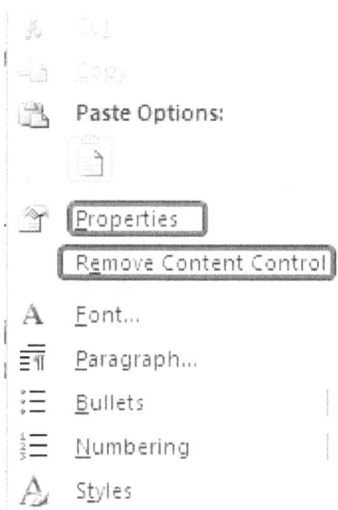

6.   **Note:** The above selections are from right clicking on the form field. As to The "**Remove Content Control**" selection that sits under **Properties**. Remove Content Control will allow you to **completely delete** that **particular** field if you so choose to. Okay, so back to the Content Control Properties.

7.   The **Title and Tag** do not, for our purposes, "have" to be filled out for us to effectively use this. If you do, that title **will appear in the bar** that you will see **across the top of the control**. Above I put the words "Enter Your Name" and underneath you will see what it looks like. Just like you had the ability to add help text in the Legacy package that appeared in the status line window below, you now

have the same ability to add instructional text that will appear on the actual Field as you see below:

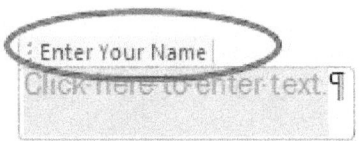

I will later on in this chapter, show you how to also spruce up the **surface instructional text** that currently says "Click here to enter text". I will show you how to add color, and manipulating the text for marketing, logo color, company color purposes but the main point is that *if you place something in the "Title" area it will guide the recipient of the form. This will hold true for anything we cover*. Also, in Chapter XIII, we will also go over some **more of the options** in the Text Form Field Dialog Box so let's just go through this piece by piece.

8.   So, back to our form. I want this particular text field to **underscore** when the recipient types in the text, so I am going to take advantage of the "**Use a Style To Format Contents**" selection of the dialog box. This is a nice feature that will let me make a **Character Style** which I will show you how to do and to then use that character style and have it **attached** or **embedded** within that particular **Text Form Field**.

Lets make a character style called "Underscore". Under the Home Tab, and under Styles (to the right) click on the little box.

9.   When the right side panel opens up go to the bottom of the panel and click on the "**New Style**" button.

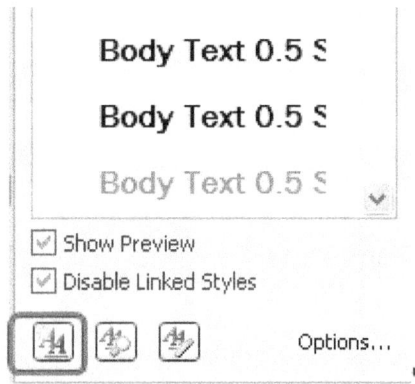

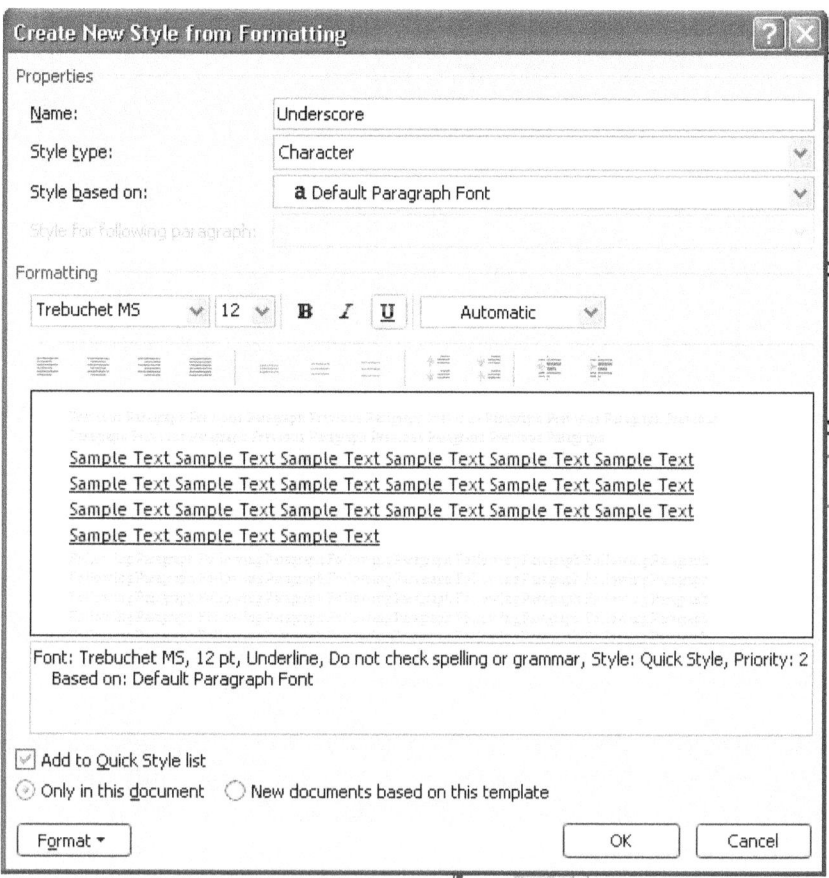

10.   Note how I filled out the Create New Style Dialog box. Style type is **Character**. I put in the **Font** and **Font size** I am using and the attribute which for this character style is **Underscore**. So now, press **OK** and we are ready to use it in our Text Form Field.

Content Control Properties [?] [X]

General

Title: [   ]

Tag: [   ]

[✓] Use a style to format contents

Style: [Underscore   ▼]

[A New Style...]

Locking

[ ] Content control cannot be deleted

[ ] Contents cannot be edited

Plain Text Properties

[ ] Allow carriage returns (multiple paragraphs)

[ ] Remove content control when contents are edited

[OK] [Cancel]

11.   Note that under the Text Form Field Control Dialog box, I have placed a check next to "**Use a style to format contents**" and have gone into the down arrow and **chose my style** that I **just made** called **Underscore**. The style is now part of and programmed into the actual Text Field. Your field code should now look like the one below. *It is important to note that this is not affecting the surface text of the form field but will take effect when the recipient clicks on the form field and starts to type their info in*.

[Click here to enter text.] Note that the Underscore aspect is now active in my form field since you see the underscore to the left of the word "Click".

12.   At this point, it is ready to go, meaning, you can lock the form just as we did with the Legacy form types and test it or send it out to the recipient etc. but, I am going to go one step further and place some helpful spruced up **surface text** in the form field instead of just leaving it saying "**Click here to enter text**. So, follow along with me and let us have some fun.

13.   If you remember, our first area that needed the text, it looked like what you see below:

This MULTIFAMILY MORTGAGE, ASSIGNMENT OF LEASES AND RENTS, SECURITY AGREEMENT AND FIXTURE FILING (as amended, restated, replaced, supplemented, or otherwise modified from time to time, the "Security Instrument") dated as of _____, is executed by [IF BORROWER IS AN ENTITY: _____, a

14.   Not only are we going to place our New Text Form field with our embedded underline style, but I am now going to show you how to do **surface text** that instructs the recipient what we want placed in that field.

15.   Again, I am going to bring in a new Text Form Field and assign my Underscore character style to it. If done correctly, as you see in the Form Field below, you should only see the Underscore before the "C" in Click. If everything is underscored then you accidentally turned **on** your underscore button. <u>U</u> . If that is the case, simply turn the underscore button **off**.

16.   Now, that the initial stuff is out of the way, I want you to take your cursor and place it before the "C" in Click.

17.   Put in the words "**TYPE IN DATE**" and make sure you bold it like I did. At this point, it will look like what you see below. Also make sure that when you type the words "**TYPE IN DATE**", that your underscore function <u>U</u> is not on.

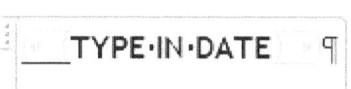

18.   Now go to the grey text that says "Click here to enter text" and back it out carefully so that your field now looks like the one below.

19.   Finally I am going to use my highlighter to give an even better look for the recipient. So, hang in there with me. You will see where I am going with this. Highlight (select the text) from the "T" in TYPE to the "E" in DATE.

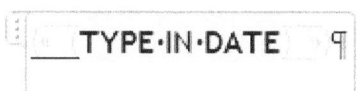

20.   Go to your highlighting area under the Home Tab ^{ab} and hit the current highlighted text with yellow highlighting.

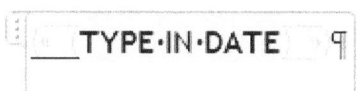

21.   Within the context of the piece of the agreement that I used as an example, it will look like what you see below **after** you have **locked** the document and tested the form by **typing in the requested info.**

This·MULTIFAMILY·MORTGAGE,·ASSIGNMENT·OF·LEASES·AND·RENTS,·
SECURITY·AGREEMENT·AND·FIXTURE·FILING·(as·amended,·restated,·replaced,·
supplemented·or·otherwise·modified·from·time·to·time,·the·"Security·Instrument")·
dated· as· of· March· 28, · 2015, · is· executed· by· [IF· BORROWER· IS· AN· ENTITY:·
_____,·a¶

22.   So, in order to test this, let us again go through the routine if you still do not know it automatically.

A.   Under the Developer Tab turn off the **Design Mode Button.**
B.   Click on **"Restrict Editing"**
C.   Choose **No. 2 - Editing restrictions - Filling In Forms.**
D.   When the prompt for password comes up, simply say **okay** since we just wish to test this.

E.   Go over to the Text field that says ___**TYPE·IN·THE·DATE** and type in your date. When you are done you will see what you see in the "MULTIFAMILY MORTGAGE" paragraph below.
F.   Once you test the form(s) click on Restrict Editing (if the right side panel is not already up).
G.   Click on **Stop Protection.**
H.   Go back to editing your form.

J.   **Remember!** I do not have to spruce up the surface text if I do not wish to. I can **simply** place an instruction in the **Title Area** of the **Text Field Dialog Box** or any Dialog Box and **that instruction** will **guide** the user. I show you the highlighter yellow method simply because people are visual and sometimes they respond better to seeing color and bold prompting but there is nothing wrong with simply putting in instruction in the Title Area of a particular Dialog Box.

This·MULTIFAMILY·MORTGAGE,·ASSIGNMENT·OF·LEASES·AND·RENTS,·
SECURITY·AGREEMENT·AND·FIXTURE·FILING·(as·amended,·restated,·replaced,·
supplemented,·or·otherwise·modified·from·time·to·time,·the·"Security·Instrument")·
dated· as· of· March· 28, · 2015, · is· executed· by· [IF· BORROWER· IS· AN· ENTITY:·
_____,·a¶

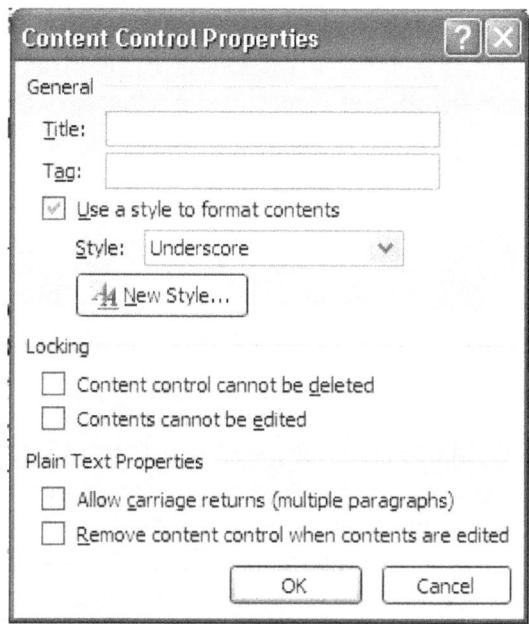

XIV.   IMPORTANT NOTES CONCERNING ITEMS
IN THE CONTENT CONTROL PROPERTIES

1.   A couple of notes concerning **Content Control Properties for the Text Form Field**. Under "**Locking**" we see "**Content control cannot be deleted**" will **prevent** the recipient from deleting a particular form field. Our goal is to have them fill out the form. If the recipient is one that has a learning curve with technology then Lock the Control from being deleted by the recipient.

2.   **Contents cannot be edited**. It seems to do exactly what it says because when I make a text field and I check this, it will not let me enter anything so I do not think you will be using this much.

3.   **Allow Carriage Returns (Multiple Paragraphs)**. If you have a Plain Text form where the recipient is going to have to put in text that will be substantive and can go on for a few paragraphs then allow them to make carriage returns. **IMPORTANT TO Note:** You **will not see this option** in the **Rich Text**, Text Form Fields simply because *it always has this option* already built into it.

4.   **Remove content control when contents are edited**. This selection deletes the field placeholder, after the user enters content into it **leaving just the plain text behind** and there is **no longer** a Text Field.

This·MULTIFAMILY·MORTGAGE,·ASSIGNMENT·OF·LEASES·AND·RENTS,· SECURITY·AGREEMENT·AND·FIXTURE·FILING·(as·amended,·restated,·replaced,· supplemented,·or·otherwise·modified·from·time·to·time,·the·"Security·Instrument")· dated·as·of ___TYPE·IN·THE·DATE ,·is·executed·by·[IF·BORROWER·IS·AN·ENTITY:- ___TYPE·IN·ENTITY·NAME ,·a ___ENTITY·TYPE ·organized·and·existing·under·the· laws·of ___TYPE·IN·STATE]·OR·[IF·BORROWER·IS·AN·INDIVIDUAL:- ___MARITAL· STATUS ,·a·[married][single]·individual],·as·mortgagor·("Borrower"),·to·and·for·the· benefit·of ___ENTITY·NAME ,·a ___ENTITY·TYPE ·organized·and·existing·under· the·laws·of ___TYPE·IN·STATE ,·as·mortgagee·("Lender").¶

5.   So just as I did earlier on in the book for the Legacy section, above, you see what the form will look like using the new Text Form Fields. Note that I went out of my way to make sure that each of my fields had personalized instructional prompts and color for the user of the form. Both the Legacy and the newer fields work fine. It comes down to preference. I have even used both legacy and the newer forms within the same form. I decided to spruce up the forms but I could have **just as easy** just placed **text in the Title area of each form field dialog box** for guiding instruction.

6.   Important: When it comes to **resetting the forms** in the **Content Control** package, it does not have the same **Reset Button** as we find in the **Legacy Forms**. So, I did find an individual (Mr. Maxey) who wrote a macro to clear the forms in the Content Control package. I will include the macro so that you can check it out and test it. You would use this if you tested the form and had placed text within many of the form fields. If you do not have a macro to clear the forms so that you can go back and edit the document with a clean slate, I usually just make use of my **Control Z** function which is the **Undo button** so that I **get my text form fields** back to their **original state** before I added my "**test**" text.

Here is the Macro that will clear out your fields if you should so choose to use it: Place the macro text under the Development Tab, go to **Macros (left side)**, the macro name is **ScratchMacro** and then press **Create**. When you press create, you will see the following come up (on the following page).

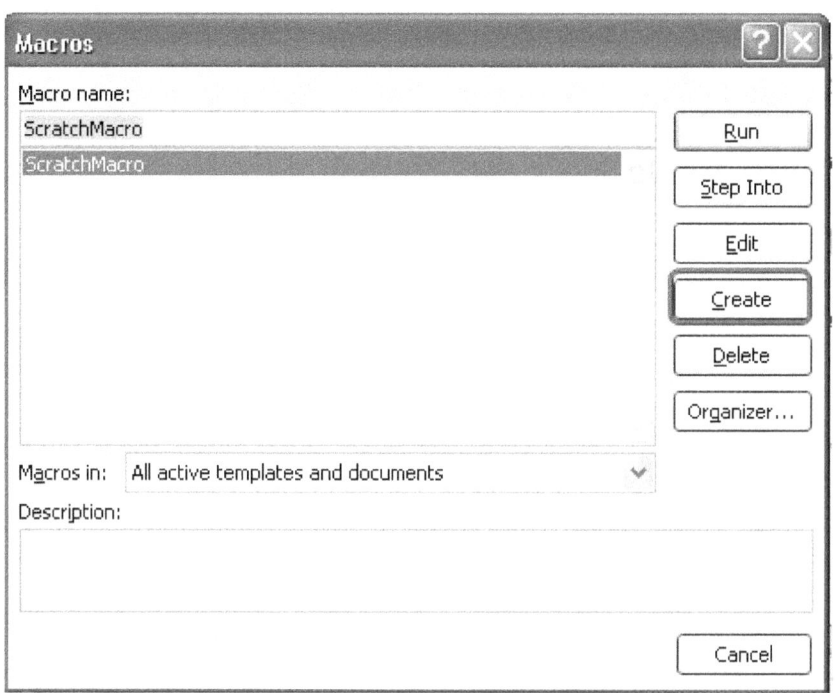

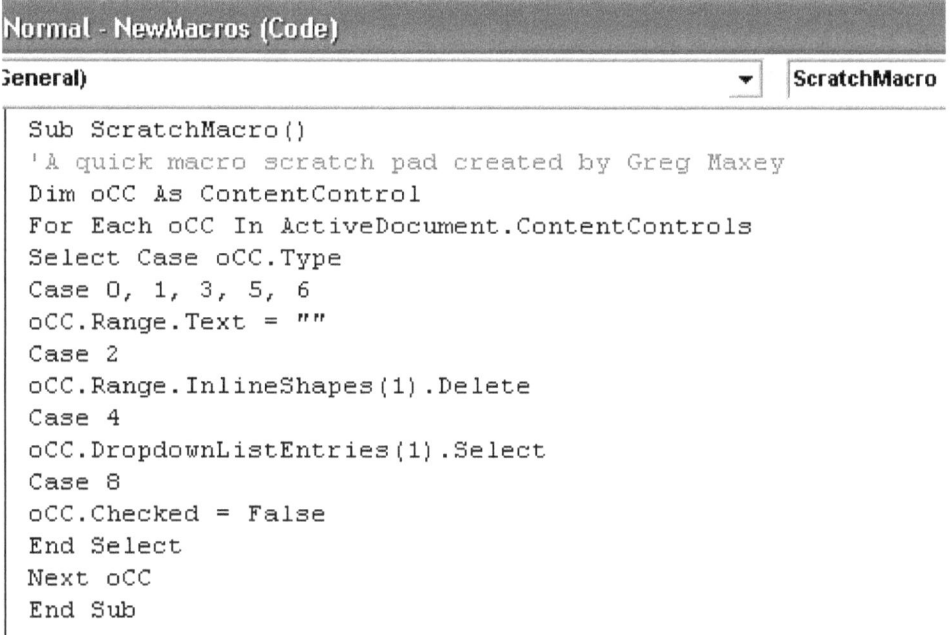

```
Sub ScratchMacro()
'A quick macro scratch pad created by Greg Maxey
Dim oCC As ContentControl
For Each oCC In ActiveDocument.ContentControls
Select Case oCC.Type
Case 0, 1, 3, 5, 6
oCC.Range.Text = ""
Case 2
oCC.Range.InlineShapes(1).Delete
Case 4
oCC.DropdownListEntries(1).Select
Case 8
oCC.Checked = False
End Select
Next oCC
End Sub
```

HERE IS THE MACRO TEXT THAT I PLACED IN THE MACRO CODE WINDOW ON THE PREVIOUS PAGE:

```
Sub ScratchMacro()
'A quick macro scratch pad created by Greg Maxey
Dim oCC As ContentControl
For Each oCC In ActiveDocument.ContentControls
Select Case oCC.Type
Case 0, 1, 3, 5, 6
oCC.Range.Text = ""
Case 2
oCC.Range.InlineShapes(1).Delete
Case 4
oCC.DropdownListEntries(1).Select
Case 8
oCC.Checked = False
End Select
Next Occ
End Sub
```

7. Finally, some very important points. When I made use of the **Plain Text and/or the Rich Text content control** I found the following. If I made use of a **style**, then I essentially **locked the user into typing text in a certain format** such as all the text is underscored or the text is bold etc. Now, let's talk about both the Rich Text Content Control and the Plain Text Content Control. If I **do not use a style**, then the recipient basically types text that takes the form of the default text of the document.

8. When it comes to the surface text (instructional aspect) of the Text Content Control Field, I am able to do whatever I want in terms of just freely typing plain text, bolded text or italicized text for the surface text or, as I told you, I can simply type text in the Title area of the Content Control Box and that can be a quick solution as well for the purpose of prompting the recipient through the form.

XVI. THE CHECK BOX

Let us take a look at the new forms check box.

Seating Type¤	Selection¤
Front·Row·Seating¤	☐¤
Main·Level·Seating¤	☐¤
Mezzanine·Seating¤	☐¤
Balcony·Seating¤	☒¤

Above, I show you a very simple use of the new forms field check box. Let us take a look at the properties section of the text box.

Again, I can get to the properties of the Content Control Check Box by clicking on the Check Box Form Field, going to Developer then going to Properties.

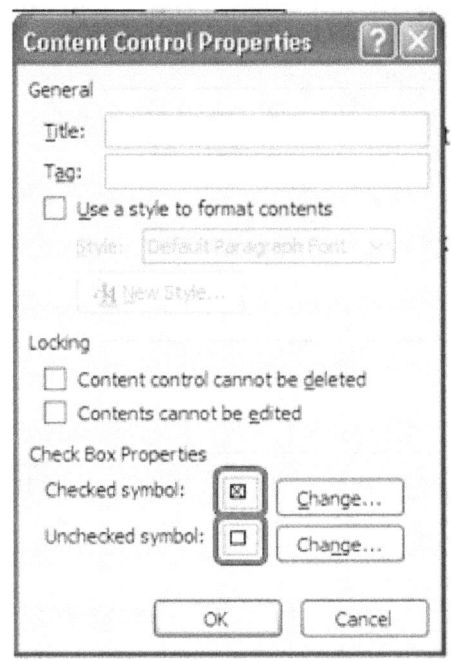

1.   Above, we see that we have the ability to **set a style** for the look of the item that is to be placed in the **Check** box such as we had the ability to do so in the Text Content Control Properties. Note that in the "**Checked Symbol**", controls you have the ability to change the symbol to whatever you wish to have it look like when you select a check box area.

2.   When you click on **Change** you get the **font maps** as you see below

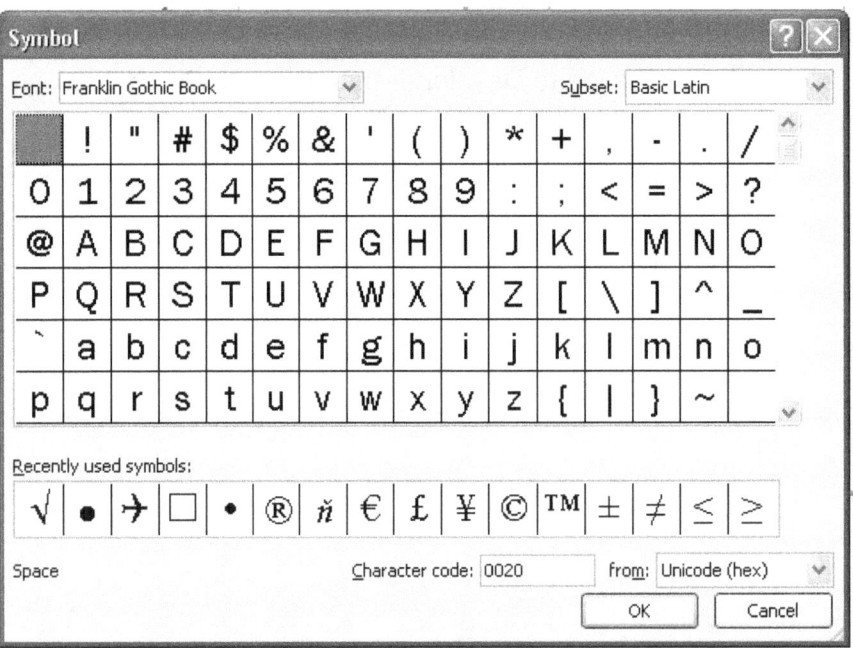

3.   If you decide to change the symbol that will be placed in the Check box I would first make sure that you **switch over** to the **font map** that **matches** the current font that you are using in the document. Most people will either use a check × or √.

4.   The reference to changing the "Unchecked symbol" is interesting but unless you have some special situation **I would leave it looking like an unchecked box**.

XVII.   COMBO BOX CONTENT CONTROL

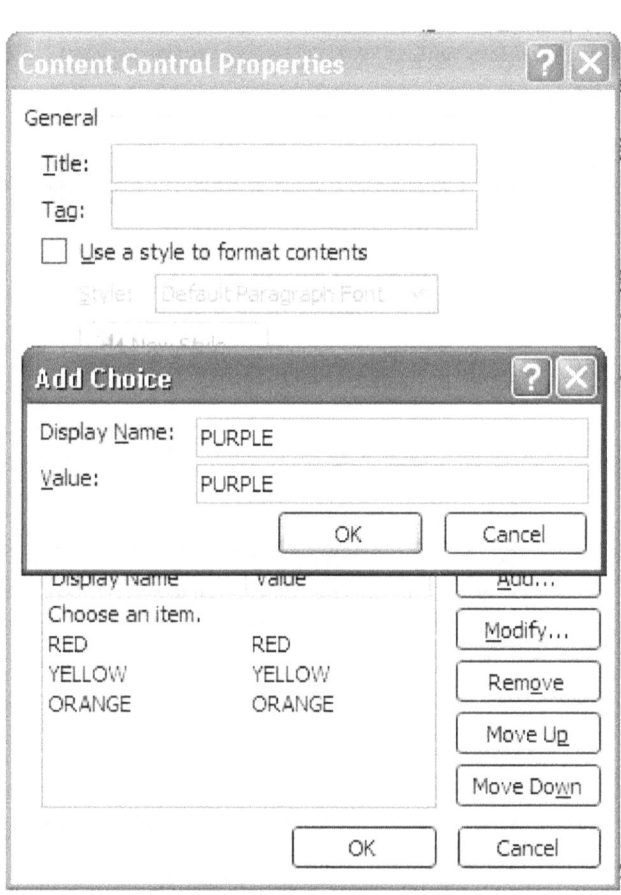

1.   We see that we have the option to use a **style** to control the look of the text that will appear in the Combo Box drop down menu. That style can be a font type, bold, italic and underscore or color. It should be noted that when I make my choice from the drop down menu, I can, with the **Combo Box Content Control**, then type other things as well such as choosing the choice of Yellow and I can then type Size 42 for example. If I don't use a style embedded within the Form Field, the look

of the text of the drop down menu will simply take on the look of the default text of the document. If I use the **plain** Drop Down instead of the Combo, then I am locked into simply picking from the list and that is it.

2.   Placing the items in the drop down is easy. Click on **Add** and put in the item and say **OK**.

3.   As you see below, I added **surface text** that was **bold** and I added some Yellow highlighting to the "**on the surface**" directions of the **Drop Down Field**. **To Test the form:**, 1) click **off** Design Mode Button, 2) Click On **Restrict Editing**, 3) Choose No. 2 and if you are not sending this out, **don't key in a password** just say **OK**. 4) Check the Form, see if it is working and when you want to get back to your document to continue editing it 5) click on the **Stop Protection** button under the **Restrict Formatting and Editing** Panel.

4.   When your recipient of the form clicks on the down arrow that will appear when they come across the **Drop Down Menu**, it will look similar to what you see below.

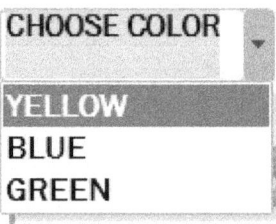

5.   If you wish to be inventive, then the form that you send to your customers, recipients etc., the **surface instructional text** of each form can be colored with your firms **colors** or **corporate logo colors**. For those of you who are marketers by nature, you will certainly understand what I am talking about. You can color the surface text, you can use the highlighting to your advantage, and you can make use of attributes such as Bold, Italic and Underscore. Note below, the colors of the mock company are blue white and yellow and I mixed them all into my instructional text of my field code.

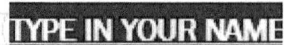

XIX.   THE DROP DOWN MENU

Okay, so let us now talk about doing a simple drop down menu.

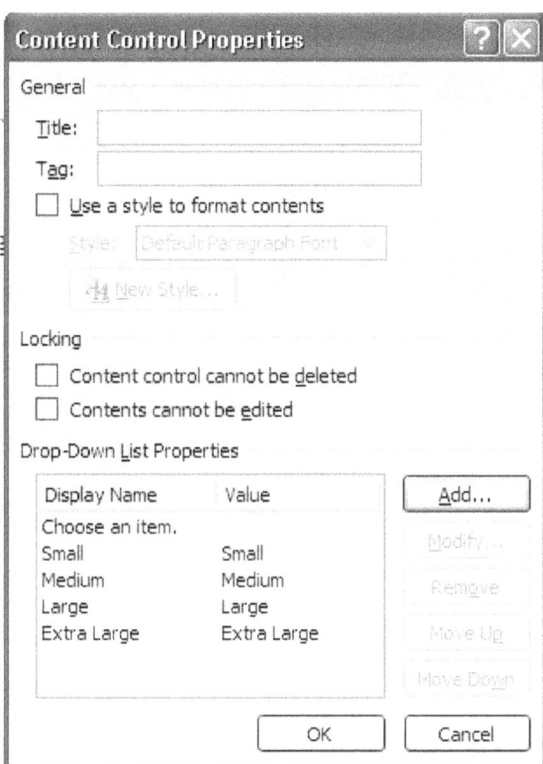

1.	Let's look at the **Content Control Properties**. We have the ability to use a **Style** to **format** the contents. As with the other Content Controls we can control the look of the text by use of a style. If not, the text will take the appearance of the default font.

2.	Adding the items in the drop down list is easy. Click on **Add**, put in each individual item and press **OK**.

3.	Unlike the Combo box, you cannot add additional text. You can make your selection from the drop down list and that is all.

4.	Once you put in the items for the Drop Down List, you can test it as well as any other Form Field items that you have in your Form Document.

5.	1) Go to your **Developer Tab**. 2) Click off **Design Mode** if on., 3) click on **Restrict Editing**, 4) Click on **No. 2 Editing Restrictions "Filling In Forms"**, 5) click on **Yes, Start Enforcing Protection and just say okay instead of putting in a password**, 6) Go through your forms and make sure they work, 7) To undo the protection, Click on Restrict Editing (if the Restrict Formatting and Editing is not already up), 8) click on **Stop Protection** and go back to editing your Form Document and finally 9) **undo** (Control Z) anything you placed in the forms as a test or **run the macro** I have provided for you in this book to clear the forms back to their original condition before you had placed any "test text" in them.

XXI. DATE PICKER CONTENT CONTROL

The Date Picker will display a calendar for the recipient to be able to choose a date.

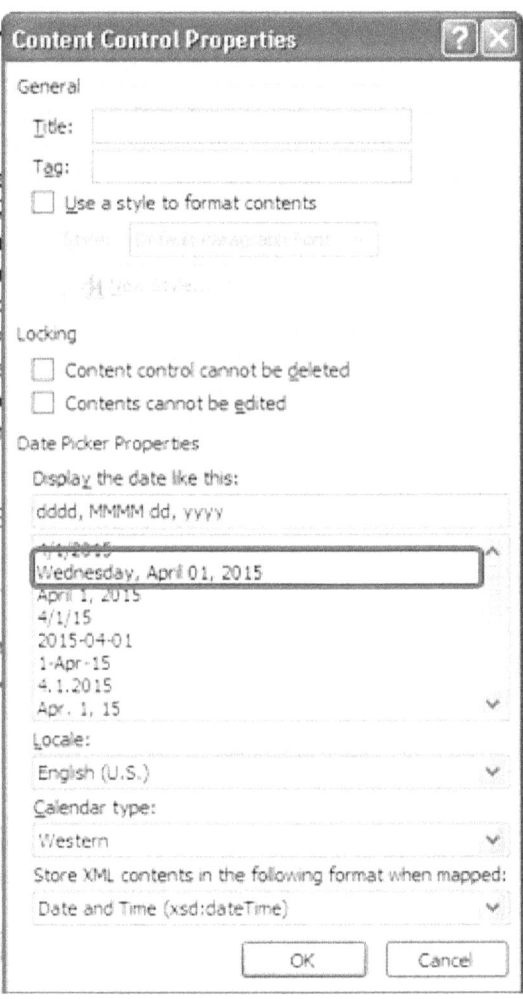

1.   As you can see above, I have made the choice of how I want my date to look when I choose it.

2.   When you **lock** the form and approach the **Date Picker Form Field** you will get the following:

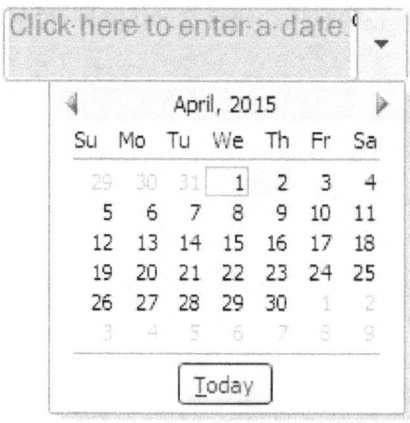

3,   Above is the Date Picker calendar that comes up.

XXII.   PICTURE CONTENT CONTROL

1.   Let us now talk about the Picture Content Control and I will attempt to give you an example when you might use this feature within your fillable form. **Example:** We are about to join a service that lists businesses online. You are going to fill out an application that asks your name, address, business address, what type of business you are in, your hours of operation, your hourly rate and at some point in the application they ask for your photo so people can place the name of your company with a face or a photo of your storefront etc.

2   When you lock the document for testing purposes and click on the Picture Control, you then get taken to your hard drive or where ever you then browse to in order to select the picture you wish to fill the Content Control Box with.

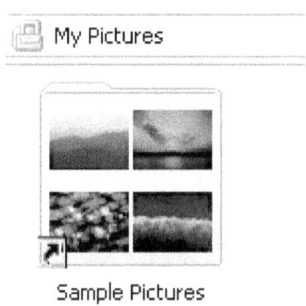

Sample Pictures

XXIII.   BUILDING BLOCK GALLERY CONTENT CONTROL

This feature will insert a placeholder from which the recipient can select a building block from a gallery that you specify.

For our purposes, I will give you an example.   Someone is filling out a Mortgage or other document.   There are different scenarios if the borrower is an individual, vs. a married couple vs. a corporation.   So, maybe we want to have a certain paragraph that can be plugged in at a specific location by the sender depending on what the category the recipient falls under.

Before we go through the steps to create a quick BUILDING BLOCK I want to create 3 small paragraphs for the 3 different scenarios.

A.   I am a prospective Borrower who is an individual, with a FICO score of 650 or more

B.   I am a prospective Borrower who is married where upon my spouse will be equally liable for the repayment of this mortgage.

C.   I am a prospective Borrower that is a corporation licensed to operate in the State of New York and has been in existence for over five (5) years.

Now that I have my 3 paragraphs for my scenarios let us make our Building Block.

1.   Highlight the first piece of text.

2.   Click on Insert Quick Parts

3.   Save Selection to Quick Part Gallery

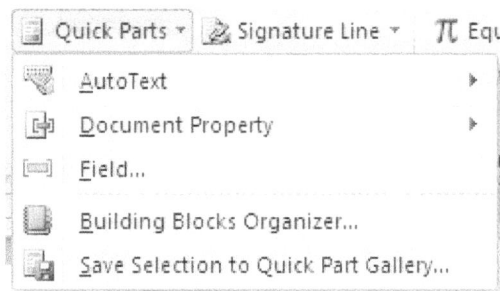

4.   Notice how I filled out this Dialog Box

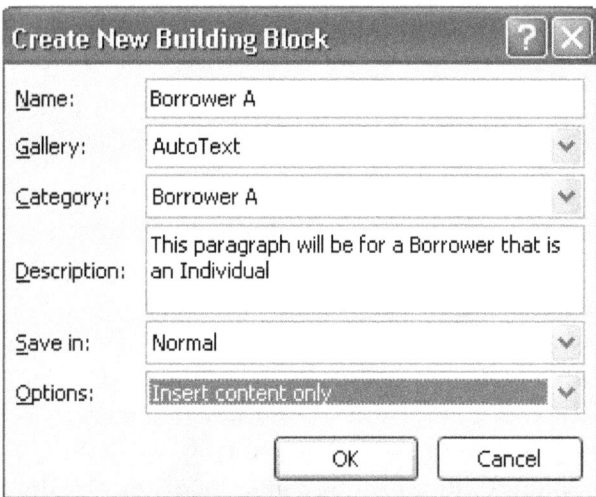

5.   Now that we have our 3 pieces ready to go let us bring in the first building block.

Choose a building block.

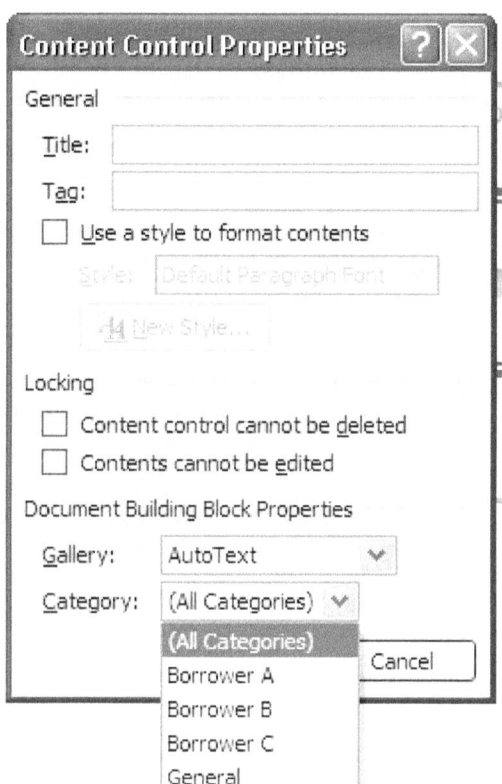

6.   Note that in the Content Control Properties above, of the Building Block Content Control, the Gallery Name that I placed my scenario pieces in is called **Autotext** and when I created those three entries, I placed the three scenarios under the Categories Borrower A, Borrower B and Borrower C. Depending on what I need for the recipient I just have to make the selection. I can also set up other building blocks with other scenarios throughout the document that give me a lot of flexibility in tailoring a particular fillable form before I send it to a client.

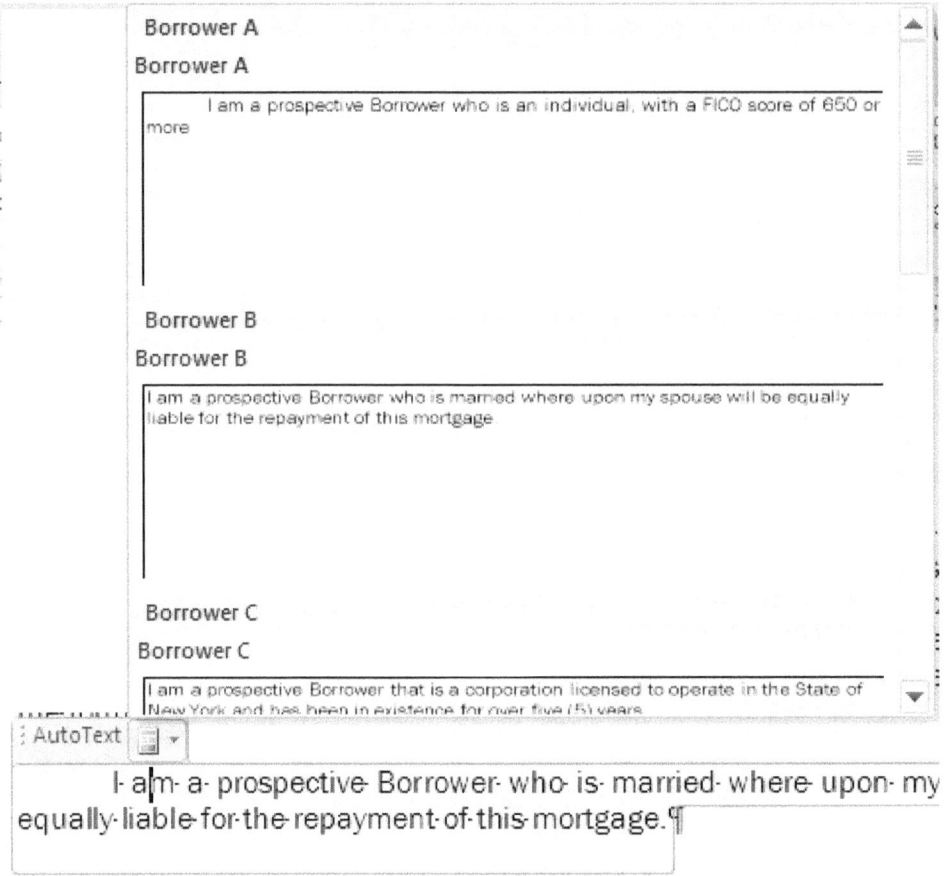

Borrower A
Borrower A

> I am a prospective Borrower who is an individual, with a FICO score of 650 or more

Borrower B
Borrower B

> I am a prospective Borrower who is married where upon my spouse will be equally liable for the repayment of this mortgage

Borrower C
Borrower C

> I am a prospective Borrower that is a corporation licensed to operate in the State of New York and has been in existence for over five (5) years

AutoText

I· a|m· a· prospective· Borrower· who· is· married· where· upon· my equally· liable· for· the· repayment· of· this· mortgage.¶

7.   Notice that depending on what my scenario is, meaning, in this case, "a married individual who called me about the Mortgage," I will now be able to select that specific Building Block that fits the scenario. For this person, the proper language that fits his scenario gets plugged into the form. Once I lock the form, the proper scenario gets locked into place but the recipient has the ability to still type within that form field in case he/she has to place their name or other pertinent information having to do with that scenario. The point is that when the block of text comes into the form the recipient will be able to edit if needed.

46

XXIV.   A WRAP UP FORM

What you see below are just some suggestions of what you can do with each selection from the new set of forms. Here is a simple custom Form with no fancy anything for a mock item that a prospective customer was to fill out. Just to show you how easy it is to quickly build the pieces of a form.

Please·Enter·Your·Full·Name:¤	¤ Click·here·to·enter·text.¤	¤
Enter·Your·Age:··(*Make·it·Numbers· Only*)¤	Click·here·to·enter·text.¤	¤
Your·Size:¤	Choose an·item.¤ ▾	¤
¤	Choose an item. Small Medium Large	¤
¶ Color:¤	Yellow → ☐¶ Blue → ☐¶ Green → ☐¤	¤
The·Date·You·Wish·to·Come·In¤	Click·here·to·enter·a·date ¤	¤
Please·Enter·Your·Photo·for·I.D.· Purposes:¶ ¶ We·look·forward·to·meeting·you:¤		¤

XXV.   CONCLUSION

So, we come to the end of the beginning. Now that you know what all of the pieces can do in both the Legacy and the Newer Content Control Package, the best thing to do is to use it. Go through making forms of all types. Have fun doing so. Make mistakes and learn from them. The more you do the more comfortable you will get.

There will be times when you want to be creative with on the surface colors and other logo or company color approaches as I showed you. Other times, you will want to go very straight forward and basic. Pay attention with each Dialog box of the particular form you are using what you can do and cannot do.

In those scenarios where attaching a style to the newer form fields will help you to mold the look of the form use styles. They are easy enough to select within the Form Field and to create as needed.

No one is perfect right off the bat. Practice, go back over chapters, feel free to contact me at louisellman@gmail.com. We are always glad to help. Our main goal with this book was to make you comfortable enough that if you are in a work scenario that you would have a comfort level that would allow you to survive to create a form in Legacy or the newer Content Control when called upon to do so. We also wanted to make sure that if you are a business owner that you have the ability to take care of your own fillable forms as needed. This will surely save you some money.

Thank you very much for buying this book and we wish you all the best.

Louis

The Low Cost Empire Series.

www.ingramcontent.com/pod-product-compliance
Lightning Source LLC
Chambersburg PA
CBHW080612180526
45168CB00007B/2879